BY A LAKE NEAR A MOON

FISHING WITH THE CHINESE MASTERS

Is A Rose Press
2020

BY A LAKE NEAR A MOON

FISHING WITH THE CHINESE MASTERS

poems by DeWitt Clinton

Poetry

Book design: Jacob Palm
Cover design: Dale Houstman and Jacob Palm

ISBN 978-0-9896245-7-2

Is a Rose Press publishes poetry, experimental writing, hybrid and other work. We are a cooperative editorial board of writers in the virtual world. Submissions are by invitation only at this time. Check our website for updates and changes in this policy.

IsARosePress.com

Is a Rose Press
Minneapolis-Missoula

Acknowledgments

Some of these poetic adaptations first appeared in:
Cha: An Asian Literary Journal, Verse-Virtual, Verse Wisconsin, The Missing Slate, Poetry Speaks: Madison (Wisconsin) Museum of Contemporary Art, Diaphanous, Qarrtsiluni, Peacock Journal & Peacock Journal Anthology, World Enough Writers: Beer, Wine and Spirits Anthology, The Arabesques Review, The Poet by Day, Poetry Hall, and *Broadkill Review*. Thanks also to the University of Wisconsin-Whitewater for a sabbatical to imagine and develop this manuscript.

Author's Note

These poems are improvisations /adaptations based on the Classical Chinese poets, Tu Fu, Mei Yao Ch'en, Ou Yang Hsiu, Su Tung P'o, the Poetess Li Ch'ing Chao, Lu Yu, Chu Hsi, Hsu Chao, and the Poetess Chu Shu Chen, in Kenneth Rexroth's translations, *One Hundred Poems from the Chinese* (New Directions: New York, 1971).

For Jacqueline

READING TU FU

1

After Reading Tu Fu's "Banquet at the Tso Family Manor"

Tonight we're having eggs again,
But we've found some plump
Tiny tomatoes to add some
Color, and of course, some taste.

The wind howls as we swirl
The eggs. There is no brook
By our house, only a frozen
Lake as big as a state.

Tonight we might watch
Another episode of "NCIS"—
I can almost say their lines
Before they say their lines.

Then, our room is dark.
The Siamese will find a
Way to nestle between us.
Tomorrow it will still be winter.
I will go home soon.

After Reading "Written on the Wall at
Chang's Hermitage" by Tu Fu

Today we are not freezing by the Lake.
The Fox News weatherman tells us
Again about the January Thaw,
Though most of us are puzzled
It ever happened this way.

More of us are now walking
On the paths and now we see
A face inside the great coats.
I like the sound of tires
In slush the way the snowy

Water sprays, and soon
Is not there. By night
I will return home, still
Safe to see you. This morning
You left as a dancer in

Blue, yesterday as a
Bumble bee. I know the
Storm is coming but I'm
Always stunned when it
Blows on me all at once.

I can nearly always find
Where we once were
But sometimes I am
Lost too long, and forget.

3

After a 10.3 Mile Winter Run, Coffee & Oatmeal
at Alterra on the Lake, I Open to Tu Fu's "Winter
Dawn" on January the 14th, Late Morning

Empty oatmeal bowl, empty scone plate, empty
Coffee cup stacked at the end of this table
After a long 29-degree morning run at sunrise
Along the Lake. At 63 I wave to everyone
Especially the motorists along Lake Drive
Who do not kill me. Sometimes I feel
The ice beneath, yet somehow
I sail safely to the next dry patch.
In the harbor, away from the floating ice,
Mallards and buffleheads wait patiently
For February. They won't leave.
I'm deeply grateful to still be here.

From an endnote on Tu Fu (713-770) by Kenneth
Rexroth: "I have chosen only these...poems that speak
to me of situations in life like my own. I have thought
of my translations as, finally, expressions of myself."

4

Mid-morning Mid-January Reading Tu Fu's
"Snow Storm" in a Ford Focus

I take some solace in Sirsasana
But I can't balance long. Nothing lasts
That long. I forget all the songs
I've ever sung, even those when
I was state soloist. I do like the look
Of an empty Pinot Noir, or Grigio.
We've agreed to keep the house
At 65 at least till April. I wish I could
Hear you more as all I hear are whispers.
Sadly, I've stopped writing letters.

5

After "Visiting Ts'an, Abbot of Ta-Yun"
before Seeing "The Book of Eli"

Sometimes I can sleep through the night
But usually someone is up either with
A "Dr G" autopsy flickering through
My dreams or someone walks through

The house waiting for light to appear.
Above us, the stars whirl by oblivious
To any of us sleeping or
Searching for the last star in space.

Every Wednesday after silent meditation
And before asanas, we chant the Patanjali
Invocation. Slowly the Sanskrit starts
To make sense to some of us.

Waking even before the radio wakes
I wonder where I could walk to today.
The dog droppings are still thick.
Perhaps I will go to the cemetery.

6

After a 32 Mile Indoor Bike Ride Near the Great Lake I
Wander into a Library and Find "Moon Festival" by Tu Fu

Nearly a month after Winter Solstice,
The Northern constellations are hidden
By overcast clouds and the dim light
Of January. Yesterday, on a long run,

Over 1000 mallards and buffleheads
Gathered in a cove off State Park Island.
I do not know where they spend nights
Or if the moon shows the floating ice.

I would invite them all home for lunch
But I'm unsure of their winter diet.
Their blacks and blues and greens
Are so brilliant against the white.

We are still at war, and will be.
The same moon lights our way
Where the enemy hides
In the cold caves of Tora Bora.

7

With Scattered Snow Showers and Winds Predicted at
10-20 m.p.h. I Find a Sunlit Window by the Lake and
Open in Delight, Tu Fu's "Jade Flower Palace"

With a heat index above 100
I catch a bus for the Forum

And Coliseum in hopes of walking
Beneath the Arch of Titus.

The winds only add to our suffering.
I buy a watercolor for my wife

Who is cooling off nearby.
Who dreamed of this hot tourist spot?

Most of the Via Sacra is now gone
Now just dust with little shade.

No togas, no laurels, no chariots,
No Roman numerals just the quiet

Suffocating heat and temples
For the old gods and emperors.

In the shade of the Arch
I look up and see robed Israelites

Straining under the great weight
Of the Second Temple's Menorah

Lost forever but sealed in stone.
Titus could not conceive so many

Menorahs lit all across the world.
Whatever we want never lasts.

8

Late January with Overcast Sky

Remembering the Walks Through
The Women's Barracks at Birkenau,
I Wonder into a Glass Enclosed Library
In the Village of Whitefish Bay and Find
Five lines of Tu Fu's "Travelling Northward"

By the 27th of January, the Russians arrived
At Auschwitz and liberated the ashes
And bones of what had been left.
The sky was so thick no bird could fly,
Except for the lice that refused to take flight.

9

In Late Morning January Light, in the Red Room Facing East,
I Open to Tu Fu's "Waiting for Audience on a Spring Night"

> & wonder if I've ever stayed up
> That long for something to happen.
>
> Outside, the flowers breathe slowly
> Underground. I haven't seen or heard
>
> A sparrow in weeks. Above, in bright
> Light, the constellations hold steady
>
> At least for now. The whole night
> Is full of movement that I can't see,
>
> Even the lonely walkers with their
> Red-tipped cigarettes & white breath.
>
> I wish I could make this a painting.
> I am not disappointed, but not surprised
>
> When I awaken from sleep. No special
> Guest has ever knocked on our door.

10

Sitting in the Waiting Room at the Dentist's Office
On the Milwaukee River I Find with Great Comfort
Tu Fu's "To Wei Pa, A Retired Scholar"

Whenever I visit old friends
From school days it's never
That good as we tell the other
What we did but not what we did
With each other. "This 'n that.
Then we saw the Grand Canyon,
And little Bobbie saw the ocean
Waves for the first time."
It's worse than watching slides
At Uncle Henry's when we were
Kids. Blah, blah. Saw, saw.
Why did we move away?
Each of us will never ask
As it hurts too much.
Even if we had stayed put
We would have drifted as
Comic books & our Mothers'
Meatloaf won't last forever.

We open a fine red, start
Sipping, reminiscing. The night
Is all stars. We can hardly
Stand so we help each other
Out onto the porch with more
Trips back to "remember when?"
Your yard is all black black
Then we see a star blazing
Across the Winter Circle.
This is what I cherish. I'm afraid
To ask if you will. Do you even
Know why I am here with you?

We open another Merlot.
Somehow I must find a way
Home, perhaps by boat if I don't
Have to steer, where I'll find
A stack of student papers
That I must grade, very soon.

11

At the Bayshore Mall, I Read the News, Then Join
Tu Fu with his "By the Winding River I"

The Dalai Lama urges us to treat
Each other as a good friend[1] but
Everyone is not. If I no longer
Smash Daddy Longlegs spiders
In our home, why would I do
That to you, or anyone?
For weeks I've been setting
Old pants out by the curb
As they slip too easily off my
New hips. The plumber finally
Plunged our sewage away.
Believe me, I am so relieved.
If I retire, promise me we can
Walk in every park in Paris.
The lamp that lights what is
Here for you is fused to
Brass bamboo. The morning
Sun glistens off the holiday
Lights of a young tree rising
Out of the concrete, and it
Must be spring, even though
It is 25 degrees. Please let
Me savor this life a little longer.

---

[1] Ethics for a New Millennium, 2002.

12

After 9.5 Miles of Indoor Running, Fatigued, Hungry,
Rested, & Filled with a Bowl of Oatmeal, I Find
More with Tu Fu's "By the Winding River II"

Mallards and Canadians descend
Onto the slippery patches of the Lake.
Food is more scarce now, just inches
Below the crust of the frozen waves.
The bouquet you bought at Pick 'N Save
Brought spring into our home, only the petals
Are falling each minute and will be gone
Before you leave. In Lake Park, the
General has not moved, ever, from his
Guardian stance. That's where we last
Saw our Angela[1] before she slowly wound
A noose to say goodbye from a rafter.
Lately, huffingtonpost.com offers more
Tips on how we can all be happy.
Away from work, does anyone suspect
I'm home writing lines from Tu Fu?

---

[1] Angela Peckenpaugh, Milwaukee poet, 1942-1997

13

After Hip Openings with Iyengar Yoga I Drive my
Wife Back to Forward Dental on the Milwaukee
River and Wait with "To Pi SSu Yao" by Tu Fu

With a child who's not adopted
And one that didn't grow, we'll have
No descendants but we'll leave all
These lines of our art and scholarship.
Perhaps that's something.

The national poetry directory swells
With talent but even so, a recent film
Critic, writing about "Evictus," asked
"Who reads poetry anyway?"

We do see each other's wrinkles,
But we can pump iron, tread treadmills,
Swim thousands of laps more than
We ever did when we first met.
We even still listen occasionally.
Perhaps that's something.

I'm saving up my 100 Best
To be read through the long
Nights of shiva. Perhaps that
Will bring some comfort
Especially the ones dedicated to you.

14

Almost the End of January

Wife Away on Holiday, I Take a Long Morning Run in Snow Showers
Along the Lakefront, Then Sip Coffee in the Boiler Room of
a Favorite Coffeehouse, and Open Tu Fu's "Loneliness"

> Three ice fishermen huddle in bright orange.
> I don't want to save them.
> Gulls and geese keep company nearby.
> Few try solo flights as the snow, first dusting,
> Now comes down in big thick flakes.
> I almost took flight after a patch of ice.
> Dogs on taut leashes pass by, jaws open.
> I'm near downtown businesses, all closed.
> If I could, I might stay in the snow all day.

15

The End of January at Last

After Laundry Folded, Trash at the Curb, and Finding Food
for a week, I Rest and Read "Clear After Rain" by Tu Fu

You are still thousands of miles away, yet
Our house has not blown away, yet.
I slept in for once, and missed the Sun
Rising on the cold January Lake.
The grapes looked quite plump today,
No mold. So many mushrooms.
From our bedroom radio, I hear
A lonely solo from a sanxian[1].
I wish I could be there.

---

[1] A Long necked Chinese flute

16

After a Longer than Usual Swim, and a Shorter
Run than Usual, I Face Overcast Light and
Wonder Why Tu Fu Wrote "New Moon"

Facing the Eastern night sky
The full moon was so full.
We pressed our thumbs closer
Than ever before. It's never been
This big before. It's like a big stage
Prop. I wanted to go there, but
Only as a trip, coffee and scones
In short supply with no daffodils,
No early spring, only long dusty winters
So far away in the Milky Way.

17

After Watching a Documentary on Plate Tectonics and the
Driest Desert on Earth, I'm Surprised to Find Tu Fu's
"Overlooking the Desert"

> Sky now grey with wet fat snowflakes
> Repainting the city in glistening white.
> Here, facing the driest desert in Peru
> I hear the ice flows that will soon
> Jam the River. Now it's late afternoon
> Everything turning dim, moody, windy.
> In college, a few buddies became dedicated
> To Sandhill Cranes. All of us are still alive,
> Looking for those lonely, dangling legs.

18

Hanging in Rope Sirsasana, and Later, Lying in Supta Baddha
Konasana, I Realize How Eager I am to Find Tu Fu's "Visitors"

It's been so long now, I wonder about all who
Come for tea, and why so few find their way.
I can stand for hours next to someone without
Knowing who's there. I still enjoy our little house,
Even if I don't go down to the River. Few call
To say they're coming over. Occasionally, I say
Hello to someone, and often they don't know
How to stop. I like the quiet nights, the silvery glow
Of our bedroom. Spies, lovers, medical examiners,
Aliens, all stop by to wish us a safe and dreamy night.

19

Facing the Eastern Light Near the Great Frozen Lake
I Search for a Warm Place and Find with Comfort, Tu Fu's
"Country Cottage"

> Like an old dog I wear the same
> Black ensemble day after day.
> I've given away all my ties and coats
> But I've kept a razor for a smooth head.
> I don't miss one bit all the old homes.
> Someone else can have the busted
> Heaters, leaking faucets, running
> Toilets. Today the Arctic winds keep
> Almost everything close to what's
> Down here. I'm not even sure about
> The gulls along the wharf who know
> Fish heads will not fly out to sea today.

20

High Noon Early February

Perched Near a Window to Catch Any Winter Sun I See
Decorated Trees Planted in the Sidewalk and Wonder What
Tu Fu Would Do with his "The Willow" in Concrete

    I miss our old Bartlett, destroyed by
    Two summer rainstorms. Now each
    Fall we order a box of Bartletts from
    harryanddavid.com but I still miss
    The drunken bees swimming in the fall.

21

Sunday Afternoon, Northern Hemisphere

After Travelling 36 Miles Nowhere on a Stationary
Bike I Peer Out the Window and See Tu Fu
Sipping Wine, Composing "Sunset"

We've spent sunset on our old porch so much
We think the whole day ends right here.
Salmon and vegetables on the grill,
Wine chilling, lonely mourning doves
Roosting on the high wires, even the grass
Knows we'll have to be more patient.
Sometimes we talk until we can't see
Each other, then one of us remembers
The cool inside, and the cool touch of sheets.
Then I remember who we've lost, buried, or missed.

22

Monday morning

After 42 Laps in an Indoor Pool, I Watch Snow
Fall on the Great Lake and Find Tu Fu Writing
"Farewell Once More" to his Friend, Yen

> I swim with a new friend. Some I see only inverted
> In Iyengar. Some I wave to. Some swing clubs.
> Nearly all live inside the ether of internet.
> Some talk forever, some just nod. Some are still
> Sad about the way things have turned. Some
> Don't even think of waving or looking this way.
> I haven't finished a bottle with a friend since
> The end of the war in the East. I can still say
> Hello, how are you? but it's harder now to
> Make a new friend. At home, I wonder through
> All our rooms. In the evening, Zac the Cat sits
> On my chest, and we talk about the whole day.
> He sniffs my nose. Will I ever see any of my
> Friends again? What in the world have I done?

23

18 More Days to Go in February

With 10-12 Inches Falling All Day, I Wonder What the Forecast
was When Tu Fu Wrote "A Restless Night in Camp"

> At night, and sometimes when we are blue
> We sleep with one sheet, two blankets,
> One comforter, three or four or five more
> Thrown on just in case. Only our noses stick out.
> On the wallpaper, African animals call out
> All night long. We don't ask what spirits
> Loom behind the masks. Today, more Brits
> Die in Afghanistan, now more dead
> Than during the Falklands War.
> Last night we watched a major escort
> A private home to Montana for the last time.

24

Midway through February, Toasty Inside a Coffee Shop Across
from the Frozen Lake, I Find a "South Wind" by Tu Fu

The meteorologist reassures us
That winter is on the down slope,
Sliding as slush out into the Lake.
Patches of bare brown grass
Appear near the elms and oaks.
The ducks, many now, circle and circle.

25

The Sixteenth of February, 5:30 p.m., Still Light Out

While My Wife Leans Back for a Pilates Class, I Slip Away
To an Old Library for "Another Spring" by Tu Fu

The River near the Lake is all
White. The flowers bloom & bloom
& bloom all day long in Pick 'N Save.
The equinox is still far away.

26

More of February

After Watching Another NCIS Episode, I Retreat to my Office
to Read "I Pass the Night at General Headquarters" by Tu Fu

Every day we receive updates on the battle
For Marjah[1]. No one knows how many
Taliban have dug in, or died. Sometimes
I wonder if I've ever left my post, still
Shouldering an old rusty M16, long out
Of ammo, stuck on Hill 477[2] in camouflage.
I hate monsoons. It is peaceful where I live
By the Lake, far away from sandbag bunkers.
I haven't saluted an officer for years.
I still call everyone sir or ma'am.
I missed all the Victory Parades.
I've thrown out all my ribbons and medals.
But somewhere the frontier pass is unguarded[3],
And like Tu Fu I wait patiently for new orders.

---

[1] February 2010 NATO Operation in Afghaniston
[2] Hill 477, South Vietnam, site of American artillery/army unit overrun
by North Vietnamese soldiers in June 1969
[3] Lines from Tu Fu's "I Pass the Night at General Hedquarters"

27

Listening to Reggae, Perched on a Stool
I Open "Far Up the River" with Tu Fu

Outside robins call for mates and nests.
The cardinals' tweet is something I try,
But I still can't whistle quite as sweet.
Outside, on their way to class,
Students sob or sing or text or ring
Afraid to walk in silence in the winter sky.
Sometimes, in the late afternoon,
A UPS truck stops with a box of what
We forgot from the Amazon or maybe Beijing.

28

Running in Snow Showers I Wonder What Wonders
Tu Fu Sees in "Clear Evening After Rain"

The Sun rises over the Lake in thick
February clouds. I catch fat flakes
On my tongue. Two nude, joyously
Nude models run by in the snow.
Woodpeckers tap breakfast bugs
High in tree bark. I want to stay
For heaven's sake, but I'm miles
From home. The Sun now lightens
The brass bamboo at my coffee table.

29

On an Overcast February Evening, I Stay Up
Late to Watch Tu Fu Write "Full Moon"

Starless night, the overcast clouds float
Dark and heavy onto our little street.
A student is fished out, just below the ice.
Ice flows far from the north drift by.
We have not polished the tea set.
Both of us still surprise (us).
I prefer, don't you, quiet rooms.
Eyes closed, it's hard to tell what spins.
Every day I bend to pick up dust.
Old, but we both still bloom.
Our tiny world of breath, blinks.

30

After Much Ice and Snow Televised from Vancouver I Wonder
if Tu Fu is Dry & Safe in his "Night in the House by the River"

It is still early this far north.
The days let us live
Life in full illusion.
Outside the new snowfall,
Wet and unwanted,
Glimmers in our eyes.
In the dark we watch re-runs,
Old movies; the dead die so quickly.
Above our pine trees,
The overcast clouds,
The satellites whirl black black cold.
All over the world DP's search
For small fires, someone with comfort,
A story to dream. By day I bring
The dead back with soldiers, wives,
Newborns, elders. Please don't tell
Me you don't remember.
In this world, what we have
Keep us wide awake all night.

31

Overcast Skies, Gloomy Grey Matter, Restless, I Don't
Want to Do Anything, so What Does Tu Fu Do on a Day
like Today with his "Dawn Over the Mountains"?

> The snow in our city falls and
> Falls and falls and falls and falls
> Turning all from grey to white
> White to grey, grey, grey.
> Sometimes even the buildings
> Are lost in the fog and grey.
> Each night a hard freeze
> Keeps all in frozen February.
> I have not seen wild turkeys
> Or red foxes, or even a doe
> Only the busy chatter of
> English sparrows, black crows
> And a sky of gulls, gulls, gulls.

32

Small Winter Objects Fall from the Sky, Make Us all
Cry; inside, Tu Fu Alone with Brush, Ink, Paper, Hears
Night Noise, Writes "Homecoming—Late at Night"

I know my home by heart,
Could almost find it
Without looking, the turns
Along Lake Drive something
I've done far too long.
Often the house is dark,
One room glows where you are.
Then we make dinner,
Eat with pillows behind us.
Soon the lights will be out,
Our eyes watching the dark inside.
We're safe, we pretend, from
Murderers, rapists, men who'd
Die to know where they could
Come murder us all night long.

33

Laughing, Jogging in Knee High Snow Drifts along
the Lakefront I Imagine Tu Fu Puzzled if his "Stars and Moon
On the River" Disappeared in a Wisconsin "Snow Burst"

The River is all white tonight.
The thin dust of snow makes
A soft carpet for the foolish.
Tomorrow all of us will wonder
Why the moon glows so at sunrise.
On the Lake, a few men still
Try to coax a few blue fins
Out of the icy Michigan.
At night the blue blue black whirls
Into the dark of the Milky Way.

34

Remembering High Beams on Night Commutes,
I Read Tu Fu's "Night Thoughts while Travelling"

At night, travelling at high speeds
I sometimes crane my neck so the
Moon can shine all yellowy into my
Old blue eyes. Moon risings are breath-
Taking, a relief after moving papers
And students around all day. In the fall,
I dread the high beams reflecting in
deer's eyes, tiny moons I don't want
To crash into. *My poems have not made
Me famous*[1] but without them I might as
Well have died when N.V.A.[2] sappers
Overran our outpost, the night lit with
Tracer rounds, a Russian flamethrower.

[1] Line from Tu Fu's "Night Thoughts While Travelling"
[2] North Vietnamese Army soldiers carrying C4 explosives

35

After a Mile Swim, I Open Tu Fu's "Brimming Water"
on the First Meteorological Day of Spring

Some nights I follow
The moon all the way home.
Ahead, I see only
Red brake lights, sometimes
High white beams.
Soon I will be safe
On our dark quiet street
Relieved I'm not dead yet.
Tonight, we'll feast on fish,
Asparagus, cold wine, kisses.

READING MEI YAO CH'EN

36

After Reading Mei Yao Ch'en's "An Excuse for Not
Returning the Visit of a Friend" I Wonder, too

Friends drop by
To see friends
Or so it seems
But I'm not even
Sure the last
Time I made
Some time to
See what's up
By you everyday
I wave and nod
So it's not like
I've never stopped
By but now
That everyone's
As good as gone
I'll admit I don't
Walk through
Your back yard
And yell to see
If you're even
Here. I've lost
You, and didn't
Intend to but if
I end up at one
More wake for
One more dear
Dead child I'll
Come by you
You bet just to
See what's up
By you old friend.

37

On Returning to the River's Edge to Find my Wife's Lost
Tooth, I Wait with Mei Yao Ch'en's "Next Door"

All the neighbors we've ever
Known have died or moved so
It's not as easy to just cross back
Yards, say come on over anytime.
To the south the old professor
Laid quietly for almost eight
Whole days before a cousin
Thought of even showing up.
The new owner built a new
Wall between the two of us.
Across the street all the widows
Are buried or left in contempt
For husbands out on the lam.
To the north every month
The sign invites all who walk
By come live here, upstairs.
We know all the dogs quite well.

38

After an Early March Run Along the Lakefront I Snack
on Honeydew with Mei Yao Ch'en's "Melon Girl"

> Thank goodness I don't have to sell poems
> At the market. By late afternoon, an old woman
> Whispers, buys the whole basket. I walk home
> Happy with two fish heads, and a melon.

39

After Three Nights of Tuna Salad I Wonder How We can Go
on, then Open to Find "Fish Peddler" by Mei Yao Ch'en

Who out there can chat with someone
Who cuts fish all day? We must know
What we all want as many stand in line.
All right then, let's have a pound of jumbo.

40

Up Early to See What's Left of the Moon, I'm Bemused
when Opening to Mei Yao Ch'en's "The Crescent Moon"

> The neighborhood dogs live
> Mostly in the neighborhood homes but
> We know the dog
> Next door lives mostly out-
> Side, caged, with nothing to do
> Even if the moon is blue or
> New or just rising or almost waxing:
> All (woofing) day (woofing) all (woofing) night (woofing).

41

After Dancing with Cars Along the Lakefront Roads, I Open
Mei Yao Ch'en's "On the Death of a New Born Child"

I may have to leave unexpectedly
Like so many of us will have to do,
Not wired, not medicated, not
Inebriated, not incarcerated,
But still I wanted you to know
How much of a joy
It's been to have those few
Moments next to you.
I didn't want to tell you until now
For fear you'd think something
Else, but just know I'm blessed
Even though we're less sure
How long any of this will last
For any of us here on earth.

42

Overcast Skies, Fog, Scattered Rain Showers, Mortar
Falling from the Front Steps, Knees Aching, I Turn a Page
and Find with Some Regret, Mei Yao Ch'en's "Sorrow"

I, too, miss all our dead, and wonder
What they're doing with all that
Time. Some, I assume, have found
Their way to Heaven. Some might
Not even know why there is a heaven.
My old gadfly from Athens looked
Forward to visiting with all the dead
Soldiers and big wigs. Maybe I would
Too if I didn't think they'd all turned
To dust. No one ever makes the trip
Back for us, not even our dear friends,
Who just might warn us of what's what.
I might just go the route of ash
Rather than wait it out in an old pine
Box making friends with crawly things.
Most of us are dead, or on our way,
Though I'm not sure I'd know just
What to do if you up and left so soon.

43

Day of Daylight Savings

After Dreaming a Dream, I Can't Forget, I Smile when
Reading Mei Yao Ch'en's "A Dream at Night"

I don't imagine I'd ever
Dream you're gone as sleep
Is something I wouldn't ever
Want perhaps I'd drift away
After many long nights, but
Even then I'd prop an eye
Open just in case you'd drop
By to let me know to just let
Go by then I'd better start
Packing up the bras and blouses
And necklaces for the nice neighbors.

44

Ides of March

After a Mile Swim, I Wonder About Lake Swims in June,
then Read Mei Yao Ch'en's "I Remember the Blue River"

> After the War I wore fatigues day in day out.
> We yakked and yakked and I wept way too much.
> We ferried all the animals to a new farm in Holland.
> For adventure, we once prayed all day in Prague.
> To see the egrets, we took a guide far up the River.
> For a moment we eye browed each other, then wept.
> Some days these dreams vanish before I even see
> You over there, still here, becoming better than ever.

45

Jubilant after Watching the Sun Rise out of the
Big Blue Lake, I'm Now Despondent after Reading
Mei Yao Ch'en's "On the Death of His Wife"

    For our 40th my wife
    Wants to see Paris.
    On our 35th we held hands
    In the Uffizi and licked gelato.
    Both of us now sport white hair
    Though she's tinted red
    And I'm quite bald. We still love
    "Cats and Dogs" so I'd never see it
    If she dies for fear I'd die of despair.

46

Sitting with My Dear Wife Near the Cold Blue Lake I Open Mei
Yao Ch'en's "In Broad Daylight I Dream of My Dead Wife"

How much time do we really have with each other?
Most days we are near each other.
Occasionally we fly across the world without the other.
Mostly, we're in each other's arms.
After dreaming I look up and there you are, dreaming.
Sometimes, though, we kiss not knowing what evening brings.
What would we do when we're dead?

47

On the Vernal Equinox with Snow Showers Expected, Mei
Yao Ch'en Remembers "I Remember the River at Wu Sung"

    I don't have to remember how I drive every
    Day the same way back and forth across the Kettle Moraine.
    Every year the Fox hardens, then widens across spring fields.
    Some days I slow down, watch flocks ascend.
    Sometimes the moon rises in my windshield.
    Cranes fly so close I smile.
    In the fall, dead deer stain the roads.
    Most of the time I wonder about you.

48

After French Green Beans and Fajita Fu, and a Half
Bottle of Sauvignon Blanc, I Read Mei Yao Ch'en's
"A Friend Advises Me to Stop Drinking"

As a preacher's kid, I never drank
A lot but the Army served
Up two bottles of cold beer every
Day in Vietnam to keep us cool.
Now I'm almost a sage with
Dental bridges and canals and a smooth
Old head. I do like cold whites
Yet lately I'm counting the bottles
In the blue recycle box we
Set out by the curb.
I wonder how many is too many.
Sometimes when we're out my wife will always
Ask if I can get
Us back to where
We started out. I'm still in the mid
Range price so I haven't even begun
To find the fine
Grapes one reads about these days.
The dark reds are maybe even better
For letting the blood run
Fast and smooth, my doc
Says, so I could lay off a
Night or two confined to just plump grapes
In anticipation of that next cold crisp sip.

READING OU YANG HSIU

49

After Crossing the Milwaukee River in Late March, I Read
Ou Yang Hsiu's "In the Evening I Walk by the River"

The River flows fast with no ice floes.
Too soon for canoes, and the fish too deadly for our dishes.
The bridge gets us to work, then home, too.
All the river boats wait quietly in dry dock.

50

Wondering about a Friday Night Fish Dinner, I Look
for Advice with Ou Yang Hsiu's "Fisherman"

The ice fish houses have all disappeared on the lagoon.
Now the men stand with long poles on the bridge
Hoping for anything tasty by evening.
What I've wanted to say is almost impossible something
   you wouldn't believe
But I'm still here, high above the River, waiting for cod.

51

After a Cold Bracing March Run along the Lake, I
Find Some Warmth with Ou Yang Hsiu's "Spring
Walk to the Pavilion of Good Crops and Peace"

El Nina has kept the trees bare
And the grass is old winter grass.
Most of us are tired of all this.
All over the village
Bags of branches and leaves
Cover the front curbs.
Near the eastern walls green
Begins to push through.
We've been played by talk
Of spring for so long
Some could now care less.

52

On a Blustery March Afternoon I Sit Down
with Ou Yang Hsiu's "East Wind"

    The trees are still black as death.
    The chickadees and grackles riot at the Lake.
    Too windy for boats today.
    Thank crows the crows haven't returned.
    We watch ballet all afternoon.
    By evening tomorrow we'll look
    For Elijah to sit at Seder.

53

Sunny, Breezy, and Mild along the Lakefront, I Imagine Spring
with Ou Yang Hsiu's "Green Jade Plum Trees in Spring"

Green flyers land on our porch
Announcing spring cleaning for cleaning lawns.
Before dawn the village sweepers wash
And dry all the asphalt.
Fresh green asparagus arrives in plump
Bunches stacked like chlorophyll pencils in bins
For the locals to steam at home.
Beneath us the bugs lay
Plans for warmer times inside our
Heated homes in time to miss
Late freezes and the first rakes.
Long pants are off the college
Crowd as shorts
And flip flops appear as harbingers
Even before we see first spring finches.

54

Watching the Moon Set in the West at Sunrise, I
Welcome the End of March with Ou Yang Hsiu's
"When the Moon Is in the River of Heaven"

> The littlest house on our street
> Is the one where we find shelter from the Winds.
> By now most of my wife's
> Perfumes are only last mists.
> If she were gone I'd spray
> What's left and let the mists drift
> Into old memories of love.
> We still can swell some
> In our old delightful garden we've
> Made beneath the covers of night.
> Each day we say we miss each
> Other just before one of us must pee.
> We still can do something suddenly
> Come Winter or come Spring.

55

After Being Passed by Young Women Running at the
Lakefront, I Savor Ou Yang Hsiu's "Song of Liang Chou"

Perfume sprays float by as I pass
The Boston Store cosmetic counters.
In yellows and pinks, young girls
Perch for free make-ups and lipsticks,
Fingers texting or whispering to BFF.
They pass from shop to shop like apple
Blossoms floating back to earth.
Sometimes they stop for skinny lattes.
Their orange and blue and purple streaks
In their new hairdos might attract young
Shaved head boys. They seldom need
To check their faces in their mirrors.
Confident they own the world
And are so special, they cannot see
How sag and bags will spoil their charm.
When they stop at corner puddles
Few see who they'll be as
They step into their watery selves.
After strolling to the mall bookstore
I see all the faces of the street
Smiling back in paparazzi shots
Of young lithe smiling stars
Forever young and pouty and much
Like all the girls so wish to be
In faces of long lashes and pink gloss.
Some men we all don't want
To know will think and plan of what
They'll do just for the flattery
Of a young girl's eyelash flutter.
Let's admit we'd all love
To find the skin of some such nymphs.
Next year, if there is a next, spring
Winds might start me thinking of old youth.

56

After Reading How Poets Often Die, I Do Hesitate to Read
Ou Yang Hsiu's "Reading the Poems of an Absent Friend"

Some old poet friends are not dead
Yet. One even lives exiled in far
Away Japan. Perhaps I'll disappear
As I'm too old to be discovered
By any up and coming new
Lit clique. What part of friends
Stays in the sublime end of my
Old mind? Sometimes when I read
They've died I'd just as soon
Close the blinds and stay reclined.
Most all stayed up all night
Just to finish their new lines.
Now they've got their good books.
I do hate reading what they've
Spent their whole lives on
And I hate it that they're gone.
Sometimes I have not written all
Year and when I do I know it's
Nothing more than old oatmeal.
It's incredible how long I've
Been drawn to this poetry life
And how often I can't even
Find a word or two to make
Anew, and wonder, who turned
My brain into yummy worms?
Once I found an old Pole's
Book of lines, left the day
For nothing else except to turn
More pages all the way to night.

I never am too keen to
Reread some old medieval
Gore but I could pick out
Any poem and think it's
Something quite new. I wish
I knew what poets do.
Most men wouldn't be caught
Dead writing with short lines
Would rather count the scores
Of grown men running plays.
I told my wife the other day
How long I've been devoted
To this quiet task of digging
Through what I already knew.
So if I could I'd just sit
Right here in our red room
And gaze outside to find
What brings such joy inside.
In fact I'd take my old dead
Poet friends, and a few lines
Made last night, catch the next
Starry ride right out of here.

57

Walking by the River I Wonder What the Question was
in Ou Yang Hsiu's "An Answer to Ting Yuan Ch'en"

We're threatened with snow flurries
By the end of the night.
The ground, almost green, can barely
Push the first crocuses and hyacinths
Up from our brown white winter.
Further south the strawberries and oranges
Are nearly ruined by late freezes.
Somewhere the first spring winds will
Drop down and deliver cold boiled ice.
The neighbors keep their wolfhound out all
Night long. We won't even dream of sleep.
The two of us wink in between the barks.
Tomorrow, since it's spring, we'll buy some
Cut spring flowers just in case you
Just might think of dropping by.
If we could do anything
We'd probably have the robins in just
To bring the spring inside.

58

After Running a Half Marathon along the South Lake Shore,
I Rest All Afternoon with Ou Yang Hsiu's
"Spring Day on West Lake"

>Today is perfect with spring breezes:
>No ice, no sleet, no gale winds.
>Too soon for sailboats, the Lake's blue,
>The sky's blue appears almost painted palettes.
>Even the clouds don't threaten us.
>Everyone's still groggy before the early
>Start which some don't even know has
>Just begun. Some fall before we start.
>Though old
>I'm still spring despite the autumn deep
>Inside with old tired thighs, old
>Shoes, old shirt, even gloves on
>These old hands but I
>Surprise us all with strides so long
>Right from the start I may
>Do this in record time.
>It's spring, the start of racing season.
>(We're so impatient just to race.)
>No need to dodge ice
>Patches as green now shoots
>Up on the sandy path.
>It's spring racing with young men,
>Young women running behind each other but
>Me, my head's still into spring
>Despite the fact my cap's all white.
>I barely know a soul, few would
>Even stop to even say hello.
>Sprinting toward a record best this spring
>May just help keep old days away.

59

Mid-April, Mid-Morning, Not Middle-Aged Anymore,
I Read "Old Age" by Ou Yang Hsiu with the Lake in View

I'll admit I ache a lot
And fall asleep before it's dark.
Most letters now say thanks but no
Thanks for what took days
To hone. Each reject adds a year.
My eyes can't take the bluey screen
Too long and sitting always
Puts my legs to sleep. I'm not
Sure what thoughts I had just then.
Quiet students say I talk and talk and
Never really stop for any talk.
I do sometimes forget just
What you said just now.
I thank Mother for the love of anything
To read yet all seem much shorter
Now and when I do find something
Interesting to read
It's usually me I end up talking
To, just glad no one's
Around to see my moving lips.

READING
SU TUNG P'O

60

On a Mid-April Afternoon, Near the Banks of the
Milwaukee River, I Read Su Tung P'o's "The Red Cliff"

Sadly, it's not the Potomac so
We don't expect to see our
President float by. We do fish
Out the dead who've dropped
Their lives from our higher
Jumping bridges. Of course
The other side is all Wisconsin,
Then a river too wide to walk
Across, then stinky hogs, and
Waving corn and waving wheat,
Snow-capped mountains then
White wine land just before the
Few can sail to old Hong Kong.
For many, this is Heaven as
The dead are planted all the way.
Long ago we gathered on the banks
To remember the wedding of
Two wiccans, complete with song
And brooms and ropes wrapped
Around their wrists for love.
Only later did we learn about
The rope that wrapped around
Our dear dead bride who
Repeated what her mother
Also did with rope. We heard
She may be resting in the East.
Why do these poet friends
Vanish into ash and smoke?
The younger ones will laugh
Their heads off when they
See my hairless head, but I don't
Care a bit, just pour that right
Up to the lip while I watch
One more moon rise out of
What we call our muddy River.

61

After Long Restorative Poses in a Morning Yoga Class,
I Go Back, Again, to Vietnam,
with Su Tung P'o's "At Gold Hill Monastery"

I don't ever want to return
To what I could call home
In the Song Chang River Valley.
From there I directed cannon
Fire on wandering NVA or VC
A few klicks from the South
China Sea. On a South Florida beach
I told my wife how much
A trip back would do me good.
Old vets have made their way
There, building schools and clinics
To make something that was not
There. If I ever
Did go back, and won't, I'd have
A terrible time just trying
To find which Hill it was
Not ever having taken tours
Unless you'd call a walk
From one bunker to
The next with helmet
And flak jacket as a stroll.
We looked to the mountains
Just inside Laos
So every sunset we'd climb up
High onto our roofs
And gaze far out into postcard vistas
So peaceful we thought monks might
Find a place to chant some
Peace that we all
Wished would find its way past
Here to somewhere
Where those who knew how to
Converse could find something
Each side knew how to agree

Around some dignitary's Parisian table
Despite all the tons of napalm
Dropped low for great despair
Making those who were below
Glow like melting crispy light
Or Agent Orange which ruined every
Range of trees so we
Could simply see who's on the Trail.
I haven't slept too well
Though all the ghosts have come
To rest somewhere in the back part
Of what's left of what's up there.
Old movies bring this all back
Even though I keep loading
Old howitzers as if I'd never left.
I may not ever
Think of landing again at this old
Miserable monastery of men as nothing
Good every came from there.
I have, though, thought of travelling
Back to those spell-binding monks.

62

After Seeing a Dark Shadow on a Waning Moon, I Stay Up
and Read Su Tung P'o's "On the Death of His Baby Son"

For Angela Peckenpaugh and Edie Thornton

We're still not quite sure how it all happened.
One day they're here, a bit discombobulated,
The next, one wrapped
Around a rope, the other, overdosed,
Then a bullet to the brain.
Some close knew how all of this
Was building, but some outside the circle
Were simply shattered that these two
Were why we gathered
Quite confused in funeral lines.
I'm older now than both
And wake from sleep
Relieved, somehow, they're here
Though all we have are two memorial trees.
Both fought for years with what
Seemed daily all their highs and lows.
On the first day of each professor's
Death we all felt cut
And bruised the air exhumed right
Out of us, of course we all went
Back to work exhausted, so incensed,
So lost in making sense of who we all still miss.

63

After Cycling Near the Lake Inside a Glassed-in Room
I Open Su Tung P'o's "The Terrace in the Snow"

By the time Friday just disappeared
We were all gazing at the grey
Circling the sliver of our moon.
Somehow we thought Eyjafjallajökull's plume
Might have drifted out that far.
Now all of northern Europe
Has floating ash so sharp and hot
No one dares fly into grit like that.
Awake for hours, I open blinds
Of where we sleep when
We can't rest past the last late shows.
Outside all the birds are tuning
Up for full-fledged orchestra and chorus.
I pick up all our
Limbs and leaves and half eaten
Apples that have landed on our deck.
The light comes later to our back forest
Burning off the damp spring fog.
We can then count on
Crows to awaken all the drowsy
Dogs to push us out of bed.
The air is thick with pollen dust.
Daffs and jonquils bloom in every yard.
We've spotted big black flies
Who arrive before the tiny ants find our little home.
Pretty soon I'll be deep in dirt
So we can feast on summer.
It's too soon for sun bathing.
My legs still ache too
Much and I wonder what I'm
Doing trying to still write.
We're locking the doors more
If those murderers try to find us
Once again.

64

I Shop for Wine so the Dancing and the Singing[1] can
be that Much More Thrilling, then Unfortunately Find
Su Tung P'o's Riff on "The Weaker the Wine"

> The lower the shelf
> The easier you can drink yourself a headache.
> The thinner we are
> The more we can wrap around each other.
> We live almost as opposites.
> If we're dancing and singing, I'll probably tell myself just two.
> We've got some quarrelsome characteristics.
> The more we stay, the more we sigh.
> Sometime soon, or not, we'll see the end.
> We seldom do what the other says.
> No need to avoid
> Us, we're an Eastern flower.
> The dust and wind we bring in will keep us all amused.
> Here, no one lives that long
> But soon we'll be waving off the last ferry.
> We each have done something great
> Though now we're less inclined to be so good.
> Every time I help with jewels I steal a kiss,
> So we're still illuminating,
> Still heating something there.
> There might not be too much left after we leave
> Except some boxed bones to move around.
> As for what we wrote, somebody may find
> Some enlightened pages, but most are not.
> Some may grab what's
> Ours, but then they'd blush.
> We still put up with bad dogs.
> A glass ends the night quite well
> Even if our stars fall to hell.
> Then sometime past 10 we fall
> Into the Great Deep Void.

---

[1] "Dancing with the Stars" and "American Idol" shows.

65

April 22
11:30 am

Months Away from the Longest Day, I Sit Down to Read Su Tung P'o's "The Last Day of the Year"

Who knows if we'll really make
It to the end of even this year.
Mother always wanted to know
When her end was near, as if she
Could just pack up and hail a cab
For death. On the worse days
I'll admit I've had enough but lately
I'm starting to balance on my head
Not leaning up against a wall as
I'm usually prone to do so I wouldn't
Mind a few more years to find a still
Salamba sirsasana I. I'll admit some
Years have really gone bad,
But then the children in the neighborhood
Have started to squeal and yell more
In tune with all the barking dogs.
On warmer days day lilies will open
Up around our old paper ash and I'd
Just as soon wait to see all bloom and bloom.
And another volcano is about to blow,
Longer, higher. Who'd want to miss
That? I'm sure if I go back to work
The place will seem brand new.
But it could be true, I might fall into
The same old abyss I usually spend
Most of my time crawling out of but
Maybe I'll have a bit of panache,
Make the new year even more new.
We may be old, but as the old boys
Say after playing ball, you're never
Too old until you're cold.

66

After Reading About China's Expanded Naval Powers I Wonder
What Su Tung P'o Has to Say in his "Harvest Sacrifice"

It's been too long since
I've brought a bull to Jerusalem for a sacrifice.
Lately, I've even wondered which prayers might do
Someone any good. I could read a few from
Memory, but I even wonder if they'll do.
We're all doing with less and less but that's
Not quite what YHVH[1] had in mind.
Even those who cast off the pier wouldn't
Want to see strung
Fish flopping on the temple tiles, instead
Most of us will post a check
In lieu of smoking bulls,
Write it off when tax time comes.
I'm still not sure if this is
My neighborhood as vans keep bringing new dogs
And kids in all the time.
Lately I've been humming old "Casablanca" tunes
But few return the sad "a sigh is just a sigh."

---

[1] The Hebrew Tetragrammaton (יהוה , or Yud-Heh-Vav-Heh) is one
name of God.

67

After Cycling through the Countryside, I Slow Down
to Read Su Tung P'o's "A Walk in the Country"

It's been such a long time since I've walked
Though our little tiny Village where I live,
And walking past the buildings where I work
Might not be the same as a walk in the country—
Fewer turkey buzzards soaring, red tail hawks
Perching, and the red foxes do not come into
Our Village as much as we'd like them to.
But if we do walk in the country it's after
A long drive just to find the country where
We can stop for greens and berries, flavored
Coffees and warm apple pies. But in the fall
We take the day to drive north into
The Holy Hills, looking for autumn scenes,
Pumpkins, corn stalks, apple ciders and the
Horicon Marsh to sight thousands of birds
Who fly through, then by dusk we drive
Into the forest to find the Fox and Hounds
Our once a year old hunting grounds
For a feast of trout or salmon, missing the
Roast elk or venison or juicy pork loin.
On this night, we drink the local wines
But not enough to get so lost in the dark
On our way home to our Village by the shore.
The next day we usually count grey
Storm clouds and sight the first snowflakes.

68

Wishing We Travelled More Away from the Lake I Look
for New Vistas in Su Tung P'o's "To a Traveler"

Have you noticed, too, how friends
Don't seem to come back quite as
Often as we'd like them to?
Sometimes, it's due to all our snow.
Sometimes the spring is too lovely.
Sometime I think you'll not ever come back.
In the morning, I raise all the shades
Thinking you'll be out there, waving.
But it's been quite windy
Blowing even through our eaves.
Maybe things will change maybe
We'll just invite all the starlings in
As they add such sparkle and of course
Such song, a treat for our old cat
Who never thinks of leaving home.

69

With Tulip Trees Blooming All Over our Village by the Lake,
I Open Su Tung P'o's "The Purple Peach Tree"

It's so hard to think of death
Around here as everything in the ground is opening into full
    bloom
Though our sweet old Bartlett tree
Has now been lathed into perfect bowls.
We loved it more than anything else we'd ever want.
First, a summer storm, then next year, quite the same.
I don't think I've ever mourned a tree
As much as our wild untamed white blossomed backyard
    Bartlett.
The bees would take such leisurely baths in the fall
Making such sweet drinking songs.

70

May Day

Sitting in the Shade in a Mall by the Bay I Wonder Why
Su Tung P'o Composes his "The Shadow of Flowers"

My wife reminds me today to start sweeping away all
Of last fall's crab apples that landed on our back deck,
But I'd like to stay inside and ponder just why
The moon and then the sun
Hold me so in shadow.

71

May 3

After Swimming in Cool Indoor Waters, I Rest Near the
Lake, Ponder Su Tung P'o's "The End of the Year"

> One thousand years from now, the place we call home,
> Even the Lakefront, may look a bit different, even
> The fish might taste oiler, fishier, even a bit saltier.
> Will anyone remember when we were here,
> Or perhaps that shouldn't matter. If we did have
> To leave, forever, into exile, onto some remote isle
> With only Kalamata olives, cold feta salads and a case
> Or two of Retsina, then maybe we might linger
> For one more Leinenkugel, one more Friday fish fry.
> If we do leave, we may never find our way back,
> Just as our friends haven't found their way back
> Either. Perhaps they're just out of our view.
> Smoke rises from our neighbor's grill
> Of Johnsonville Brats. The college kids
> Across the street are pouring from a keg,
> So close to the end of their term.
> I should have done more around the house,
> Or for you, but living with Su Tung P'o
> Has had its soothing moments, too.
> Soon we'll all be quite carefree.
> In a few years, we could even fly away somewhere.
> I just can't bring back yesterday, sweetheart,
> But I'm sure we'll think of something.
> Sometimes I think we could take a nap,
> In the afternoon, maybe?

72

With Spring Road Construction Everywhere in Our Village
I Pause to Read Su Tung P'o's "On the Siu Cheng Road"

Every day it's blowing and blowing.
I cycle through the neighborhoods.
If I look up the sky is
Sometimes cumulus, then cirrus. All
Our trees are turning green from black.
Blossoms still fall on spring
Green lawns, white fences.
Pools should open Memorial Day.
All the road crews wear
Bright yellow, more yellow than the daffodils
They dig up, taken home
To their wives as bouquets
Of happy love.

73

May 6

Reading "Thoughts in Exile" by Su Tung P'o
after a Cold Ride North by the Lake

Today I sail north on black
Roads, wave at grazing caribou,
Listen to the honking geese above.
I've never known
How to climb above everyone else.
We still dream about Paris
Though it's thousands of miles away.
Away from my work
I think often of poems.
Most poets I meet
Always want the next poem.
I doubt if we ever go back home.
I hope we can see more of the world.
After all these years what is it that I know
Besides knowing all that I don't know?
After the longest ride
I'm grateful that I can
Still hear those honking geese.

74

Perched by a Window Overlooking a Mall on the Bay, I
Look Over Su Tung P'o's "Looking from the Pavilion Over
the Lake, 27th, 6th Month. Written While Drunk"

Early May and we're still freezing.
Few will walk along the beach.
No one thinks of sailing.
Further south, waves of oil wash
Into the Delta as shiny ink.
To the north, smoke and
Ash float again across
The Continent. A tanker barely moves
Across the blue sky.

75

Sitting in an old Pumping Station along the Lakefront, I Wonder
What's in Su Tung P'o's "The Southern Room Over the River"

Each week, new colors for our bed.
I usually lock the doors, close all the blinds.
Under sheets, blankets, quilt, we seldom hear the crash of
   waves.
Sometimes I drift into the TV haze.
Sometimes I'm scared, sometimes I'll dream of morgues all
   night.
We seldom sleep and snore all night.
I usually raise the heat, let light back in.
On Mondays, I make my own waves.

After Reading the Monday Obits
I Find Su Tung P'o's "Epigram"

More men are throwing lines for fish.
Beneath the waves, they've never heard of frying.
Once dead we seldom reassure
Our friends of what they've heard.

77

Homebound by Downpours, I Wait for Better Weather
with Zac the Cat, and Read to him
"At the Washing of My Son" by Su Tung P'o

> We pretend our old cat
> Can still hunt wild game even if
> He just stalks tiny ants and summer moths.
> Every day he bathes all day
> And leaps with ease to perch.

78

With the Sun Peeking onto the Lake I Open the Shades
and Read Su Tung P'o's "Moon, Flowers, Man"

We don't get many visitors who
Stop by for a refreshing cold glass yet
Every drinking night I check what
Phase the moon is in, and where
It floats in the sky
Then give a quiet thanks for joy
But more for blooming lilacs,
All breathing beasts, all legged
Creatures who speak or don't utter
A word in French or Urdu or
Any speech we might
Use to toast the night
And forget all those who
Might break in to slit our throats.
Perhaps they'd like to try a new Pinot.

79

In a Waiting Room Overlooking the Lake, I See a Bouquet
of May Flowers, and Read Su Tung P'o's "Begonias"

I bring home a yellow
Hibiscus along with groceries,
Cover it with a see
Through plastic bag so frost
Won't steal the blooms at night.
Alone on the porch next to the snow
Shovel, rusting table and chairs,
The raccoons pause before the light
Surprises them with blooms and eyes.

80

On a Mild May Day Near the Lake I Read
"Rain in the Aspens" by Su Tung P'o

> My neighbor across the fence prunes
> Her row of Bartlett Pears
> Which once would pollinate ours.
> Looking out our forest window
> Late at night her lights
> Shine right through our bedroom.

81

Near the End of the Academic Year I Take Time
to Read Su Tung P'o's "The Turning Year"

> Each day that passes clouds
> Come by as cumulus or nimbus.
> With spring rains, The Deep Tunnel fills with our waste.
> Tonight, we want to dance and sing at the Maharaja.
> My mother always asked, how long do I have, son?

82

After Swimming Indoors Near the Lake, I
Rest with Su Tung P'o's "Autumn"

The lakes are still too cold to take long swims.
The weeds below are warming up.
Flowers will soon start to droop.
The spirea is almost all white.
I hope I have the memory to remember this spring.
The longest day isn't far away
When grilled meats smoke all day long.

83

After a Long Training Ride Along the Lake I Sit
Back and Read Su Tung P'o's "Spring Night"

On this cool spring night, we watch
One more dancer who's not a star.
At the last ballet of the season
Children offer plastic bouquets to the divas.
Now that it's spring our neighbor's caged shepherd always
woofs and woofs.
In our forest among the lilies
Our old cats sleep beneath the stones.

84

After Seeing White Spring Cycling West from the Lake,
I See Su Tung P'o's "Spring" is Our Spring, too

Bridal wreaths are blooming everywhere.
The white buttons make beautiful boutonnières.
Spring winds lift the branches into floating air.
Across the city the spirea wave like fronds.
Soon the white disks will float into snowflakes.
How many of us will see this next year?

READING THE POETESS LI CH'ING CHAO

85

After a Spring Evening of Baked Cod, Green Beans
and Cold Wine, I Relax with "Autumn Evening
Beside the Lake" by the Poetess Li Ch'ing Chao

Each day the Lake is warmer and warmer.
Each day more and more bathe on the beach.
Each day boats arrive from dry dock.
This weekend, the beach house opens.
White sails already billow in the harbor.
Winter is boxed away until Labor Day.
In a few days millions of girls will vote
   for an "American Idol."
Older folks will have a new star on "Dancing with the Stars."
Park painters have started to paint the swimming pools.
The forsythia has six yellow blooms.
River crews are cleaning the river trails.
The sea gulls provide aerial complaints.
A body has popped up where ice
Fishermen once sat all day.
Another fell in last night, tipsy.
Young men and women, muscled,
Are starting to crew down the River.

86

After Watching *Rigoletto* on a Sunday Afternoon by the Lake, I
Look to See that Li Ch'ing Chao has Composed "Two Springs"

Summer sales are everywhere in town.
Our uncut neighbor's lawn launches a billion dandelions.
The crabapple trees are starting to snow
On our dandelion free green lawn.
Above, puffy white clouds make
Shadows on some of those below.
From our basement Zac the Cat
Appears in a new spider web veil.
I'm quite hesitant to keep on dreaming
As the ones at night bring on a sweat
And the ones when I'm awake make
Those close by ask where did I just go?
Where we are the moon rises
When we've already latched the house.
We keep trying to return
To whom we were so long ago
When we sprang from bed like startled deer.
We still know what brings delight
Despite all our efforts otherwise.

87

Waiting in a Starbucks Near the Lake, I Read *The Times* then Find "Quail Sky" by Li Ch'ing Chao

It's almost time for iced tea
Instead of the usual half decaf.
I'm usually the first to open blinds
To let the sun back in.
The green leaves of fading flowers are even
Drooping to the ground.
Some spring mornings I'm down
On the beach thrilled to watch
The sun rise out of our Lake.
With days like this I'm eternally
Grateful just to see what's next.
I miss, though, all the friends
I've ever made who never
Think again of dropping by.
I'm in the back
Down on my knees pulling
Weeds so tomatoes
And broccoli and maybe even
Blue Egyptian iris can cheer us some
In this tiny spot
We still call home.

88

After Swimming in an Indoor Lake
on the First Day of June I Wonder, Under Water,
about Li Ch'ing Chao's "Alone in the Night"

On Memorial Day, every gardener gathers
Lots of flats of flowers and vegetables
To go quickly into small patches of black earth.
Knee dropping to pull weeds, I join neighbors
In our late spring rites. Inside, my
Poems still need help from an old
Drunk who knows better than I
How to break those lines.
Do my poems ever change who you
Still are, or do you
Just smile and nod sometimes?
By early night I'm fast under
Covers scared of even more murderers
Who'll come to murder us.
Lying in a grave
All night long maybe I'll dream
Of women carrying lanterns for their lovers.

89

On a Warm June Saturday, I Wonder How to Hum "To the
Tune, 'Plum Blossoms Fall and Scatter'" by Li Ch'ing Chao

After you're gone, you're White Linen mist
Floats in our tiny bedroom.
In the evening, west winds
Lift our curtains with big breezes.
I can't recall when I last
Read something about what love might be.
Have you noticed the yellow finches?
Once, the moon filled our bedroom.
The rabbits have feasted
On all our baby broccoli plants.
The rains pour off our
Roof into our green secret forest.
Does a day ever go by
When I don't wonder where you are?
Some days I'm on the other side
Of the world, and then, I wonder
What color amber you might
Wear someday, or not.
While I'm alive I'm always wondering what
The two of us might do sometime.

90

On a Cold, Rainy, Rainy Day in June, I Try to Find Solace
with "The Day of Cold Food" by Li Ch'ing Chao

In six days, I will swim
In cold cold waters of Lake Elkhart.
The outdoor grill needs cleaning
From all of last year's
Feasts of fish and vegetables.
Tonight, we'll dream with just one pillow
As we've stored all the rest.
The red-tailed hawk has not
Stalked our back forest all day
But we know what his taste
Is for garden-fed rabbit.
It is much too cold to scull
Down the river or swim
When rain pours all day.

91

After Completing an Olympic Triathlon Under Overcast Skies
I Rest in Dry Clothes and Read Li Ch'ing Chao's "Mist"

Every morning we let the forest
In with light and birds into
Our tiny bedroom.
We keep our blinds
Closed all night in fear of
Who's hiding right outside pretending
To come in with lonely knives.
Every day low flying jets
Make booms over the Lake.
We let the evening breezes cool
Our papered elephants and sleepy tigers.
We've replanted so many broccoli plants as
Briar Rabbit noshes on our young.
We'll sit in sunset to catch
Every single moment.

READING LU YU

92

Nearing the Longest Day of the Year, I Pull Weeds, Plant a
Flat of Flowers, then Open Lu Yu's "The Wild Flower Man"

No one really notices the old woman
Who sells bunches of bok choy
In the shade outside the indoor palace.
All morning long we never see
Who hoes and chops all day.
They've been here since the War
Brought them across from old Laos.
The marigolds and asters always
Sell before her leafy greens.
The two of us wonder where they
Go when they're not behind what
We love to smell.
We've both been down on our
Knees (as well) pulling all the weeds we
Just don't want to see in-
Between what we've planted that we hope
We'll grill along with just caught fish.
Our good neighbor just
Can't stand the woofs woofs anymore
So we'll see squad cars
Pulling up late at night to check
Out what's not right with our
Doggy neighbor who by now
Is smiling with a cold one.

93

After a Long Run Along the Lakefront, I Try To
Nap with Lu Yu's "Phoenix Hairpins"

For days our kitchen blooms with yellow day lilies.
Wine glasses hang for more cold wine.
Outside, all over the city,
Chrysanthemums are starting to open. Above us
Clouds turn dark blue into thunderstorms.
Soon the mailman will come carrying
More rejections once again.
I sometimes wonder if I'll ever
Find what others already see.
What does it matter if everyone
Chatters on about what they've just
Done to keep pain
From drifting back in all over again?
Clothes no longer fit the featherweight
I've slimmed into but the yellow
Daylilies have opened in our village
Soothing what I can't do myself.
I'd like to be here
When there's no more time
To let this ink seep into something
That you might want
As something precious, forever.

94

Thinking about not Returning to Work I Read Lu Yu's
"Leaving the Monastery Early in the Morning"

At night, I'm so dead
Even murderers stay away.
Zac the Cat sleeps
In the forest on my legs.
By dawn usually
I find coffee and news.
Soon my sabbatical will end
Though I'm not quite ready
To greet young minds
Who may wince when
Seeing someone so old.
Tonight, it's beans and wild vegetables
That will help me find
My way back to trouble.

95

After a Stormy Summer Night, I Read
"Rain on the River" by Lu Yu

We rent a houseboat and motor
Up the Mississippi until dusk.
With little practice, we take aim
At a sandbar for the night.
None of us can fish
So we break out the whiskey.
We watch satellites whirl across
The top of the sky, sleep
Until fish start jumping through dawn fog.

96

After Sprucing Up the Yard Some, I Read "Evening
in the Village" by Lu Yu in the Shade

By the evening sunset our little
Village becomes sleepy
Except for the dogs on guard.
I'm a bit tipsy on cold
Pinot. Soon the moon will rise
Up from our great Lake.
All my hopes and wants
Are buried beneath old day lilies.
No one calls anymore
To hear what once was wisdom.
We sold our horses years
Ago so now I just herd cats.

97

After an Early Morning Run along the Lakeside, I Rest Old
Legs with Lu Yu's "I Walk Out into the Country at Night"

I seldom think of walking all night
But perhaps I could walk
All the way to downtown then
By morning be on the border.
At night the trees would sway
And make the saddest sounds.
At night singing
Travels further since we
Can't tell where the voices started from.
By now I don't know why
I'm here, not home
In bed with covers keeping murderers away.
It's like this every
Time I'm driving home so late
With only our moon to guide me
All the way back home.
My wife's still up with her insomnia.
Then we're both in bed
And the night stays right outside.
Tomorrow we'll be so much older.

98

After Watching Fireworks from a 55th Floor by the Lake
I Fall into a Relapse, Find Solace in Lu Yu's "Idleness"

We keep the front door locked
In case aliens show up
Wanting to fix up our little place.
Road crews remind us it's summer.
We're lucky living with Lake breezes cooling
Us down on our warm summer days.
Sometimes my wife will read
Something new in the world of health.
We wonder if we'll live longer.
Every now and then I'll walk
For a new bottle of wine.
In our forest, I've planted
Food for rabbits and us
As well as purple day lilies.

99

After a Summer Lightning Storm, I Read
Lu Yu's "Night Thoughts"

> I do not make the dark
> My business as I'm much
> Too done in by the day.
> If I do stay
> Up I'll let the quiet
> Sounds of air conditioning whirr
> And the old cat's pacing lull
> Me back into the quiet of the night.
> It's about the only time I'm still
> Enough to hear what really
> Goes on when I'm not
> Around but drifting back to sleep.
> I'm not so sure I want to ever
> Travel back to my old
> Days of robbery or dying in some
> Hospital in some meningitis epidemic.
> I'm not sure if
> Those days were ever happier than now
> So why would I go back?

100

After Keeping Company with a Noisy Fly All Night,
I Find Comfort with Lu Yu's "I Get Up at Dawn"

I am slowly disappearing, so soon
Old friends will have trouble seeing who's
Inside what was once robust me.
In the morning at the wash basin
I look twice to see
Old skin hanging close to bone.
The hair, if there, would be grey
By now and the eyes look slightly
Retired though inside I'm quite alive.
In the evenings, I sip cold wine
And slip my fingers over old
Friends I've read and sometimes,
Pull down to smile all over
Again, even if some are gone.
I still smell the old
Love poems of ancient Greeks
And wonder why I cherish them
Despite the me who's almost gone.

101

Leafing Through an Old "People" Magazine, I Turn
Instead to "Autumn Thoughts" by Lu Yu

It's hard not to pay
Attention to the young
Russian sitting outside
The village coffee house smoking
Through two packs since I
Stepped in, but she's
Oh so much more
Famous in my eye just
Sitting knees to chin her
Smoking nose unnoticed by who might
Walk by not even
A glance or
Sense the earth might spin.
We're as good as vanished.
Winter's still not here.
Tonight we dine
Out on our wedding day.
We dream of strolling soon
In faraway Granada.
It's not that hard to climb
The bluffs to see our Lake.
I'm learning how to run
The 95 steps behind our
Lake Park Bistro.

102

After a Training Run Along the Lake I'm Surprised
With Lu Yu's "Sailing on the Lake to the Ching River"

Signs along our beach remind swimmers
Not to even dream of going in
To float with sewage flows.
Along the Lake I pace
Myself with all the local soaring gulls
Who seem to swoop
Much faster than I can.
The village road crews stay
Much longer than we'd like them to.
Everyone at the Lake
Stands in line for custard.
The lifeguard rows and rows all
Afternoon weary of those who wade in.

**READING
CHU HSI**

103

After Watching Cyclists Race along the Lake
Front, I Return Home to Lie Down, and Nap
with Chu Hsi's "The Boats Are Afloat"

Last night two more men rise
To the surface of our Lake.
On Sunday afternoons, white sails
Dot the Lake's far horizon.
In an inland lake, I swim just above
Weeds turning my head to sky, weeds, then sky.

104

Reading "Spring Sun" by Chu Hsi on a
Warm July Afternoon Near the Lake

After noshing on tuna with peas
We step out into our garden forest to check on
Our 30-foot-long pumpkin plant.
On these humid days
We're grateful for breezes that may come our way.
Yesterday our Village almost floated
Away with more rain than ever
Before so we are all steaming.

105

On a Warm Summer Night I Stay Out in the Forest as Long
as I can and Read Chu Hsi's "The Farm by the Lake"

The only part of nature higher
Than us are the clouds
That float by each season.
We've seen almost
Every cloud in the book.
In our forest, we lean
Back in our lounge chairs
Cooling our lips with tea.
When we do have a
Full moon all our
Neighbors lean over our fence
And we forget, briefly, what woofs
Day and night behind our green crops.
We've said to each other how
Much we'd like to stay until
There's nothing left of us.
There's no place we'd really like
To visit more than this place.

106

After Reading the Morning's News Near the Lake, I
Turn to Chu Hsi's "Thoughts While Reading"

The 22-inch screen gleams back
At who we are, reclined.
It's a mirror of splendor
With dancers, murderers, chefs and "X-Files"[1]
All acting as special guests.
We've even learned how to save their future
In case we're not here, now.
Summer storms often change our little stage to black.

---

1 A once popular TV series that featured two F.B.I. agents who
searched for paranormal activity and the possibility of an alien-human
conspiracy, now in reruns.

READING
HSU CHAO

107

After Watching How Blow Flies Convict Another Murderer,
I Read, with Heartache, Hsu Chao's "The Locust Swarm"

In our youth, we'd never even think
Of reading about those who "passed on"
But for several years now we've
At least glanced at locals
Who've had someone write up
Something nice to say.
Of course, they died with wounds
Or were struck down or taken or
Left so unexpectedly or fought valiantly.
We see quite enough bodies laid out
In morgues so we've no need for
Close-ups of bugs or bullets or
Drawn blood but still we know
Our chances of lying out like that
Are pretty good knowing what we've
Been doing out in our old forest
Where dead pets lie beneath day
Lilies nourishing the hungry bugs below.
When the hum of cicadas come
Every now and then, I pause and wonder
If I've ever swept
Old husks or webs or legs away.
Perhaps there's room to invite all in
When the nights start to cool
The ground when just about everyone
Looks for a safe, warm, un-deadly bed.

READING
THE POETESS
CHU SHU CHEN

108

After Running in Light Rain Along the Lakefront,
I Rest with Chu Shu Chen's "Plaint"

Our day lilies droop
In the July heat.
We could flood our old forest
With water lilies and white sail boats.
As long as there's a lakefront
I'll probably run back and forth.
I've made friends with so many
Birds of colored wings.

109

On a Shabbos August Afternoon, I Calmly
Read "Hysteria" by Chu Shu Chen

The chubby face is a bit
More chiseled, maybe even too
Sunken, in places, now.
When a big wind blows
Across the Lake I try to
Batten down what almost flies away.
Soon I will not even
Be who I could have been,
But the weight of old sorrows keeps
Me right inside my grief.
Yellow crested chickadees fly right
Outside in our little forest.
My eyes have even
Started to bulge out a bit.
I'm almost like a
Trunk with lichen up and down.
Sleep comes so little
Now I no longer dream
Who I was before I killed.
I wake up in darkness
Just before light comes to the Lake.
There's still so much to do.
Tonight, we've made a cold
Meal and dine with bright Italian lights.
Neighbors smile at our little love affair.
In the forest, the white
Russian pine waves all night.
We've turned our home into a little
Heaven with creatures who mosey
Up with their glassy eyes on us.
Soon we'll have a waning moon.

110

Reading "Spring" by Chu Shu Chen after
Swimming in Indoor Water Near the Lake

It's easy to forget what I've forgotten.
Best of all, I forget all
The terror and tears that makes life
Far too bright with stage lights.
I'm not sure there's anyone I've ever hated.
I'm too inconsequential to ever feel betrayed.
On Yom Kippur, I always want to
Wear white, ready for earth.
I still can choke on old movies.
I'm starting to shop for smaller sizes.
In a few weeks, another season begins.
I'll probably have to buckle down
And listen to complaints from new students.
By the end of the long third test,
The winds will change over the Lake.

111

After Watching Afternoon Autopsies in August,
I Read Chu Shu Chen's "The Old Anguish"

Some days, in the late afternoon,
We might nap in our cool jungle
With the Panama fan slowly
Moving across the two of us.
Outside tiny birds perch within our reach.
Inevitably, someone slashes the neck
Of someone we've never known,
Darkening our bluey screen.
What happens in our sleep
Never quite seems the same.
I'm still so relieved when we
Do awake from dreamed death.
In the evening, we sit with
Forest creatures until we're quite frightened.

112

Awake Before Anyone Walks along the Lakefront, I
Rise and Read "Morning" by Chu Shu Chen

Most of the time I'm up before
Even the birds know what's up.
I barely recognize who's who
With the ribs so prominent
Below the sinking face.
Water helps brings the body back
To where it was once
Before. I shave the head, face
Then steam the old skin.
I'm the first in our little kitchen
So I prepare food for loved ones.

113

In a Waiting Room by the Lake I Take Up
Chu Shu Chen's "Stormy Night in Autumn"

After the storm that nearly swept our
Village away, we're still soaking up
The creeks that entered our old basement.
I still hate the monsoons
That poured so long in Vietnam.
My old feet feel more and more
As if lead was pouring
Through all that is inside.
Someone's sobbing wakes me up before sunrise.
A painted face cheers us both.
Sometimes I think the night might
Just leave us in the dark.
We'd have just the wind
Blowing in on us huddled and deep beneath.
We're both more thin than ever
But not quite nimble as bamboo.
We're on the toilet more for longer runs.
Someday the rain will stop
Before it rises to our old windows.
Outside we hear the drops
Land on each green
Leaf we've ever known.

114

Alone in my Study Near the Lake I Read
Chu Shu Chen's "Alone"

On our street with so many houses
I miss the moon rising on our
Lake. By late evening we're
Already nodding off with old TV friends
Helping us through August.
Every day a new body's pulled
Floating down or up in one of our rivers.
At sunrise coyotes hunt for grass hideouts.
Our sky is filled with hungry dragonflies.
It's only now that I wonder
Where all that I've done
Has gone. Tonight, we hold
Each other so we will remember each other.

About the Author

DeWitt Clinton is the author of *The Conquistador Dog Texts* and *The Coyote Inca Texts* (New Rivers Press), and *At the End of the War* (Kelsay Books, 2018). His poems and essays have appeared in national and international journals, including *The Journal of Progressive Judaism* (with co-author Rabbi David Lipper), *Journal of Inter-Religious Dialogue*, *Cultural Studies<=>Critical Methodologies*, *Storytelling Sociology: Narrative as Social Inquiry*, and *Divine Inspiration: The Life of Jesus in World Poetry* (Oxford U Press). A few of his poems

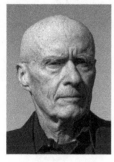

have been choreographed by the University of Wisconsin—Milwaukee Dance Department, Dance Works, and Dance Circus in Milwaukee. He also tries to balance an Iyengar Yoga practice with training for triathlons and races from 5Ks to marathons. He is Professor Emeritus of English at the University of Wisconsin—Whitewater, and lives with his wife, Jacqueline, in Shorewood, Wisconsin.

Photo by Meredith W. Watts
"For Good" Photography

About the Artist

Joan Thomasson (1935-2015) studied Chinese Brush Painting under Professor Hsiung Ju of Washington and Lee University in Lexington, Virginia, and she also studied brush painting while teaching English in 1990 at Chengdu University of Science and Technology in Chengdu, Sichuan, People's Republic of China. She was a lifelong educator of English, Science, and Brush Painting in the public schools of Albemarle County, Virginia.